The Unity of Anglicanism:
Catholic and Reformed

Henry R. McAdoo
Archbishop of Dublin

Morehouse-Barlow Company, Inc.
Wilton, Connecticut 06897

Copyright © 1983 Henry R. McAdoo

All rights reserved. No part of this publication may be reproduced, stored in a retrieval system, or transmitted in any form or by any means, electronic, mechanical, photocopying, recording, or otherwise, without the prior permission of the copyright owner.

Morehouse-Barlow Co., Inc.
78 Danbury Road
Wilton, Connecticut 06897

ISBN 0-8192-1342-1

Library of Congress Catalog
Card Number 82-62392

Printed in the United States of America

These lectures were given as the annual Theological Lectures for 1982 in the Queen's University, Belfast. The series was established by the Church of Ireland in 1956 with a view to the study of aspects of Anglicanism. The lectures are arranged by the Church's Board of Education and the Executive Committee of the Student Center and are delivered in the University by kind permission of the University authorities. My thanks are due to the Chaplain, the Reverend John Dinnen, and to the Vice-Chancellor, Dr. Peter Froggatt, for their help and for the kindness of their welcome.

Thy Church, My Care
7

Archbishop Wake and
Anglican Self-Understanding
in an Ecumenical Context
33

Notes
77

Bibliography
85

1

"Thy Church, My Care"

It is natural, because it is easier, to take one's history in potted form. We all tend to do it some of the time, and some of us do it all of the time. We dismiss or we superficially assess by means of a free and only partially discriminating use of labels for men and for movements. We are exposed to the temptation to use concepts simplistically and to use them, and the phrases encapsulating the concepts, almost as talismans, charms capable of expressing total meanings though without benefit of rigorous analysis. Such an uncritical usage often attaches to the phrase "The Elizabethan Settlement." In the minds of some, the concept is surrounded with deductions which do not always stand up to testing.

I take the phrase as an example of this kind of thing because it has direct bearing on some of the matters which I would wish to investigate in these lectures. For instance, two such implications or deductions come to mind, and no doubt professional historians will be aware of more.

In the first place, the word "settlement" is sometimes implied as carrying undertones of what today would be called "a deal." The suggestion alleged is that Anglicanism resulted from nothing more than a set intention of avoiding the extremes of Roman Catholicism and of the Continental Reformation. A rickety compromise was cobbled together with a view to holding the Catholic-minded and the Puritan-minded in an uneasy yoking. Each was accorded something and encouraged to be satisfied with peace on those terms. On the surface of things, one could find sufficient indication to give some plausibility to the idea. There was, for example, the rise in England of a national consciousness, and this new factor of nationalism linked up with the current concept of "the godly prince" to produce a stress on the Church as the Church of the whole nation. While this was true, it is not always noted that there were during the same period in sixteenth-century Anglicanism certain clearly marked parameters for the idea of comprehensiveness. Furthermore, there was an equally clearly marked and positive doctrinal direction. The heroic labors of Matthew Parker, Archbishop of Canterbury from 1559 to 1575, demonstrate that in fact an entirely different dynamic energized his efforts to bring order into the confused situation in which he had to work. He saw his Church securely anchored doctrinally in Scripture and the Fathers and he allowed no severance, but rather asserted unbroken continuity between the Early Church and the Church of England. Parker wrote in 1564 to Sir William Cecil about a conversation with the French Ambassador and the Bishop of Coutances that "in fine they professed that we were in religion very nigh to them. I answered that I would wish them to come nigher to us, *grounding ourselves (as we do) upon the Apostolic doctrine and pure time of the Primitive Church.*" The Anglican reform was the recapturing of the Catholic faith of the Church when it was, as Lancelot Andrewes put it, "at the best." Not a compromise between *contemporary extremes,* Parker would have said, but a bringing back of the *pure original* into the contemporary scene. "Protestant and Reformed, according to the Ancient Catholic Church," as John Cosin would express it later in the next century.

In the same way, the phrase "the Elizabethan settlement" has associations for some which imply that the mainspring of the whole business was somehow or other largely political. The suggestion has been made that Elizabeth I sat very lightly to religion and simply sought as ruler to achieve and preserve peace and order in her realm, and that this desire was the chief, if not the sole, ingredient in her Church policy. She has even been depicted as a humanist. Of course there was a healthy vein of humanism in her complex and sophisticated make-up—Roger Ascham surely saw to that—but it was a Christian humanism. Those who present Elizabeth as a purely political animal, a diplomat whose attitude to Church and faith was one of cool and detached calculation, will find this view modified to disappearing point if, with J. P. Hodges, they study the devotional books which Elizabeth both composed and used.[1] These are at present in the British Museum and they allow us to intrude on the inner life of a Christian ruler. Written in French, in Italian (her favorite language,) in Greek, as well as in English, the prayers reveal a humble suppliant for grace, conscious of a great responsibility to be exercised by her on behalf of others. And constantly

recurring are prayers for the Church—
"Thy Church, My Care." Petitions that
she should be given grace to "nourish
the Church" that "I may look only on
the things which are to the praise of
Thy name and the advantage of Thy
Church . . ." are numerous. The
phrasing of so many of the prayers is
that of a deep devotion and of a religion
of the heart.

The Basis of Anglican Self-Understanding

I have indulged in this preliminary note
because if we are to enter into an understanding of the fulness of Anglicanism
we need to have a critical attitude to
simplifications from whatever source.
We need to relate our formulation to
historical realities (as far as we can
apprehend them) and not to half-truths
or to myths, our own or other people's.
The modest aim then of these two lectures is to unpack certain ideas and to
see how they illuminate the meaning of
the claim to be both Catholic and Reformed which is incorporated in the
Constitution of the Church of Ireland.[2]
Is it a glory, the true vocation into
which the Anglican Communion must be
constantly striving to grow, or is there,

as John Inglesant remarked, an inherent danger in this connection as long as the simplistic concept of standing between two extremes is allowed to infect Anglican thinking at this profound level of its self-understanding?

In his dedication to Elizabeth I of his *Apologia Ecclesiae Anglicanae*, Bishop John Jewel took care deliberately to refute the accusation "that we had rebelliously withdrawn ourselves from the Catholic Church." The book appeared in 1562, published, be it noted, with the Queen's authority. In it Jewel set out unequivocally where Anglicans stand in respect of their Catholic heritage which they have recovered in its original purity through the process of Reform. It is important to stress how Anglicans at that very crucial turning-point understood themselves. That self-understanding is very far from the careless thinking which suggests that the theological *raison d'être* of Anglicanism was the deliberate attempt to steer between the extremes of contemporary Roman Catholicism and contemporary Protestantism. That Anglicanism did in fact reject doctrinal and ecclesiological aspects of both was *consequential* and not the object of the exercise. It followed as a direct consequence from what Anglicans believed Scripture and the early Church to be saying about "the faith once for all delivered." Such rejections, whether of certain aspects of the Continental reformation or of the counter-reformation, flowed from the Anglican insistence on the *hapax* and on continuity with the Primitive Church, and not from the desire to achieve as a stated objective a medial position.

This comes through with great clarity in Jewel's *Apologia*, one of the earliest, if not the earliest, essays in Anglican self-understanding. He asserted that Anglicans had not "changed anything taught and approved by the fathers, but only errors, superstitions and abuses . . . *which lawful reformation of our Church . . . is so far from taking from us the name or nature of true Catholics* . . . or depriving us of the fellowship of the apostolic Church or impairing the right faith, sacraments, priesthood and governance of the Catholic Church that it hath cleared and settled them on us."[3]

There, at the very outset of the period of separation, is a statement of how Anglicans understood "Catholic and

Reformed: the unity of the Faith in Anglicanism." Jewel further insisted that "We have returned to the Apostles and old Catholic fathers. *We have planted no new religion, but only have preserved the old* that was undoubtedly founded and used by the Apostles of Christ and other holy Fathers in the Primitive Church."[4] Parenthetically, I would observe that this is precisely the stance of the 1870 Preamble and Declaration of the Constitution of the Church of Ireland. Having asserted that the Church is Catholic and Apostolic, the Preamble asserts that the Church of Ireland "doth continue to profess the faith of Christ as professed by the Primitive Church" and that it is Reformed because it deliberately rejects all doctrinal innovations "whereby the Primitive Faith hath been from time to time defaced or overlaid." As we look at what was actually believed and affirmed at that time rather than at what some suppose to have been the doctrinal motivation of Anglicans in Elizabeth's reign, it is worthy of note that "this clear statement of Anglican credentials was issued in the name of all the bishops as a book giving their considered judgement and doctrine: Parkhurst, Bishop of Norwich, blessed it with the words *Is omnium nostrorum nomine edidit.*"[5]

Any factual assessment of Anglican self-understanding then requires that this should be carefully noted. The rationale of the Anglican position with its central assertion that any course which separates the Church of England from the Church Catholic must be rejected, is a permanent element in that self-understanding. A typical restatement of it would be that of Herbert Thorndike a century later, in 1660: "I am satisfied that the differences, upon which we are divided, cannot be justly settled upon any terms, which any part of the *Whole* Church shall have just cause to refuse, as inconsistent with the unity of the *Whole* Church."[6] No doubt the traumatic experience of the Cromwellian régime, producing as it inevitably did after the Restoration a fairly hard-line Anglican reaction, meant that Anglicans expressed the principle more self-consciously at their best and more polemically at their worst. The point is that all the time from Jewel onward, the Church of England understood itself as the representative of the Church universal on English soil. It is to this conviction that the appeal to Scripture and to the continuous tradition of Church life, *semper et ubique et ab omnibus*, is geared.

The question for twentieth-century Anglicans will then be something like this: How, if at all, does this element which our fathers in the faith held as indispensable to their self-understanding bear on Anglican thinking and attitudes in the 1980s? It is a question to be tackled not only in the interests of our self-understanding but also for the sake of our self-explanation to our brothers and sisters of other Christian traditions.

Contemporary caricatures in which comprehensiveness is treated as a synonym for compromise and Catholic and Reformed as simply the contrasting and opposed elements of an antithesis had clearly no part whatever in original Anglican self-understanding. How then do matters stand to-day when Anglicanism, now a growing and a world-wide Church, is in dialogue with fellow Christians of all the great Communions? Has time made changes in the way Anglicans see and explain themselves? Have modifications come about through alteration or attrition or new theological and ecclesiological insights?

Contemporary Aspects of this Self-Understanding

Possibly then the most useful function to be attempted in these lectures is one of analyzing and, if need be, of de-mythologizing. Such an attempt involves the separating of a whole cluster of concepts around this central Anglican appeal to the *hapax* of Scripture and to the faith and practice of the Primitive Church, as enshrined in the Preamble to the Constitution of the Church of Ireland, and in the 1878 Preface to the Irish Prayer Book, and more recently still in Canon A. 5 of the Revised Code of the Canons of the Church of England. This reads: "The doctrine of the Church of England is grounded in the Holy Scriptures, and in such teachings of the ancient Fathers and Councils of the Church as are agreeable to the sacred Scriptures. In particular, such doctrine is to be found in the Thirty-Nine Articles, the Book of Common Prayer and the Ordinal." This cluster of concepts includes, for example, that of comprehensiveness, of fundamentals and non-fundamentals, of synthesis and symbiosis, and of the specific theological method of the threefold appeal to Scripture, tradition and reason. Running through them like a thread of silver is the stress on continuity in faith and order and a concern with what one may call the legitimate limits of diversity within a given unity. Hence, the shorthand title of these lectures: "The Unity of Anglicanism: Catholic and Reformed."

On the principle of *reculer pour mieux sauter*, let us go back for a moment to 1936. In that year a young priest named Michael Ramsey published a book entitled *The Gospel and the Catholic Church.* In the course of that book, we can see how he took hold of the basic element in Anglican self-understanding discernible in the sixteenth and seventeenth centuries, and gave it fresh thrust and a wider reach by relating it to the way in which the New Testament sees the Church and the Gospel.[7] He was in fact developing in modern terms and in the specifically Biblical context what Laud had been saying centuries before. For Laud, Catholicity and continuity are not in a "narrow conclave." There is a criterion which is the determinant, and so the purpose of Laud's book is "to lay open those wider gates of the Catholic

Church, confined to no age, time or place; nor knowing any bounds but that faith which was once (and but once for all) delivered to the saints."[8] Significantly, it is the *hapax* which appears here, and equally significantly Laud links the *hapax* to the distinction between fundamentals and non-fundamentals.[9]

Broadly speaking, Ramsey's thesis, to which I have in general subscribed ever since I became theologically conscious, is that Church and Gospel are indissolubly one fact, and that the Catholic emphasis and the Reformed emphasis are one in the New Testament, or, if you like, two complementary aspects of the one Gospel of God: "For the Anglican Church is committed not to a vague position wherein the Evangelical and the Catholic views are alternatives, but to the Scriptural faith wherein both elements are one."[10] This is Jewel *redivivus*, but with a difference. Let Ramsey himself elaborate: "But, if our reading of the New Testament and especially of the Pauline Epistles is correct, these two truths—the Evangelical and the Catholic—are utterly one. To understand the Catholic Church and its life and order is to see it as the utterance of the Gospel of God; to understand the Gospel of God is to share with all the saints in the building up of the one body of Christ. Hence these two aspects of Anglicanism cannot really be separated. It possesses a full Catholicity, only if it is faithful to the Gospel of God; and it is fully Evangelical in so far as it upholds the Church order wherein an important aspect of the Gospel is set forth. To belittle the witness of the Reformers and the English Church's debt to the Reformers is to miss something of the meaning of the Church of God; to belittle Church order and to regard it as indifferent is to fail in Evangelical insight since Church order is of the Gospel. Hence 'Catholicism' and 'Evangelicalism' are not two separate things which the Church of England must hold together by a great feat of compromise. Rightly understood, they are both facts which lie behind the Church of England and, as the New Testament shows, they are one fact. A Church's witness to the one Church of the ages is a part of its witness to the Gospel of God."[11] The last sentence might be Herbert Thorndike speaking in a later time, but in the happier context of today's divided Christians seeking to gather up the fragments of their broken unity—rather than in the mutually hostile atmosphere of post-Restoration England.

Ramsey makes due allowance for varieties of thought and apprehension and for individual preference which finds certain aspects of truth in religion more appealing and satisfying than others. Given this human reality, he concludes "But there is a true and a false way of thinking of the comprehensiveness of the Anglican Church. It can never be rightly expressed in terms of Victorian latitudinarianism or broadmindedness, or by saying: 'Here are two very different conceptions and theologies, but with a broad common-sense humanism we combine them both.' Rather can the meaning of the Church of England be stated thus: 'Here is the one Gospel of God; inevitably it includes the Scriptures and the salvation of the individual; and inevitably the order and the sacramental life of the Body of Christ, and the freedom of thought wherewith Christ has made man free."[12] The final words carry with them overtones of the Anglican theological method, the appeal to Scripture, antiquity and reason, by means of which the Church is maintained in the truth of the Gospel. This is one of the group of concepts clustered around the main stem of Anglican apologetic.[13]

But before turning to an analysis of these we may remind ourselves that the kind of self-understanding at which we have been looking is not just a thing of the remote or of the recent past. It is alive and well at the moment. In a lecture given last year in Dublin, the Bishop of Woolwich, the Right Reverend M. E. Marshall, had this to say: "The renewed Church will have about it a *pleroma*, a fullness. What we in our parochial pettiness have kept in separate compartments to which we have given labels, God in his goodness and graciousness gives us above all in a new *pleroma*. But we have kept it separate, we have pared it down. The witness of the New Testament is always the same ... I believe that there are three ingredients in this fullness: sacramental, evangelical, experiential ... sacramental, catholic, yes if you like; evangelical, the Word; experiential, charismatic, though I want to be careful how I use that word. The trouble is, that we have compartmentalized: 'We're sacramentalists, we catholics.' 'We're evangelical, we preachers.' Really? I haven't noticed much of late. 'We're charismatic, we experientialists.' Really? I thought we all were . . . God is renewing the Church at a point where these three ingredients converge: sacramental, evangelical, experiential . . . each needs each other."[14]

Is not Marshall, in an immediate and contemporary context, talking about the wholeness and the unity of the faith, as did Jewel, Thorndike and Ramsey? Emmanuel Amand de Mendieta said it all when he asserted that "The fulness of Anglicanism will be utterly catholic and uncompromisingly evangelical at the same time, all of the same breath."[15] What comes through is that there is an essential integral relationship between Bible, tradition, reason and experience, in the way Anglicans receive, understand and expound the Christian faith. In his enthronement sermon in Canterbury Cathedral in 1942 Archbishop William Temple, looking at the Anglican inheritance in itself and in the context of the search for that wider unity to which he made a major contribution, said: "So let us set ourselves to gain a deepening loyalty to our Anglican tradition of Catholic order, Evangelical immediacy in our approach to God, and liberal acceptance of new truth made known to us; and let us at the same time join with all our fellow Christians who will join with us in bearing witness to the claim of Christ to rule in every department of human life, and to the principles of His Kingdom."

So let us consider some of the elements which are present and formative in Anglican self-understanding.

Comprehensiveness

This concept needs to be disentangled straight away from the notions of the caricaturists and of the alibi-seekers. The former, from outside, will tend to say (falsely, as I believe ecumenical dialogue has demonstrated) that it makes conversation with Anglicans impossible since it implies no doctrinal core. The latter, from within, may seek to use it as an alibi for "anything goes," doctrinally speaking. Admittedly, both are minorities but the notions of both are rejected by classical Anglicanism of yesterday and today. As the present Archbishop of Canterbury put it in a lecture last

March in Westminster Abbey: "It is quite alien to original Anglican thought that there could be logically opposite expressions of faith in fundamentals. To be an Anglican is not to be content with self-contradiction."[16]

In that comment one can discern at once the interweaving of two of these elements to which I have already referred, that of comprehensiveness and that of fundamentals. This will require consideration in a moment but let us turn to a modern comment on comprehensiveness from a significant source, the Lambeth Conference Report of 1968. Nor is it without significance that the comment was made almost incidentally in the course of the observations of the Section dealing with the renewal of the Church in unity. The section report reads: "Comprehensiveness demands agreement on fundamentals, while tolerating disagreement on matters in which Christians may differ without feeling the necessity of breaking communion. In the mind of an Anglican, comprehensiveness is not compromise. Nor is it to bargain one truth for another. It is not a sophisticated word for syncretism. Rather it implies that the apprehension of truth is a growing thing: we only gradually succeed in 'knowing the truth.' It has been the tradition of Anglicanism to contain within one body both Protestant and Catholic elements. But there is a continuing search for the whole truth in which these elements will find complete reconciliation. Comprehensiveness implies a willingness to allow liberty of interpretation, with a certain slowness in arresting or restraining exploratory thinking."[17]

The Implications of the Concept and its Relation to Anglican Self-Explaining

When I look at this description of comprehensiveness—and I do so critically—I find compressed in it several propositions which either turn out to resemble closely, or to bear directly on, the cluster of concepts already mentioned as belonging to Anglican self-understanding. I notice too that Stephen Sykes in his book *The Integrity of Anglicanism* detects in this Lambeth statement three elements.[18] Probably we are both critical, at some points, of this non-infallible statement, but our reactions would not necessarily be identical nor our approaches always the same. Let it be said also that this Lambeth extract is a valuable statement in that it says true things, even if it suffers by reason of compression. As in the case of this lecture, for instance, directions can be indicated but an ordinance survey map requires a large book.

The first proposition is that comprehensiveness demands agreement on fundamentals. The second proposition discernible is that comprehensiveness is not compromise and the third assertion is that it is not a sophisticated equivalent of syncretism. All three appear to me to be linked together. That which links them is the Anglican insistence on the *hapax*, "the faith once for all delivered." I would remind you here of the position set out by Jewel and endorsed by the Anglican episcopate of his day.

At least two other propositions appear either explicitly or implicitly in the extract from the Lambeth Report. These are that comprehensiveness implies that the apprehension of truth is a growing thing and that it requires at least a sympathetic relationship between authority and freedom. Involved with at least two of the elements in the statement is the practical problem, which is both ecclesial and doctrinal, of the legitimate limits of diversity within a Church (or within a reunited Church.) All this "homes" in at various points on our theme of "The Unity of Anglicanism: Catholic and Reformed" and the statement signalizes this by noting that "it has been the tradition of Anglicanism to contain within one body Protestant and Catholic elements."

Even if we may consider that this phrasing is loose and theologically rather shallow, we must grant that taken as a whole this short extract manages to bring together much of the matter which bears on Anglican self-understanding and self-explaining. This is so because behind its seemingly bland and occasionally superficial summarizing there lies a vast historical tract of a Church's continuing experience and worship, of proclaiming, teaching and living the Catholic faith by the members of *Ecclesia Anglicana* through the centuries.

As we pass in review these various propositions and their implications for Anglican understanding of the faith it seems to me that none of them can be separated at all distantly from this central concern for the profession of the whole faith of the universal Church as Scripture reveals it and as Councils explicate it and as the Creeds summarize it. Anglicanism deliberately chose this direction towards the end of the sixteenth century. It continued at the heart of Anglican apologetic thereafter and was incorporated in the Preamble to the Constitution of the Church of Ireland in 1870. It remains to the present and a question for Anglicans in the twentieth century must be, How well has the concept worn? Are there problems about this position today?

Historically speaking, it is from this center that Anglicanism has considered and formulated the idea of comprehension, maintaining that any doctrinally allowable and ecclesially workable principle of comprehension requires agreement in fundamentals. How has this been worked out?

Fundamentals and Non-Fundamentals

The application is by means of what a recent inter-Church document, the Malta Report,[19] characterized as "the Anglican distinction of fundamentals from non-fundamentals." It can at once be seen how this bears directly, though with varying force, on most of the elements which have been suggested as components in the concept of comprehensiveness. The distinction has been part and parcel of the Anglican understanding of the unity of the faith from Hooker through Laud and Taylor to the present so that to mention names is otiose. What is interesting is that it is seen by a modern inter-Church Commission to be part of Anglican self-explaining and its ecumenical potential is noted by the same Malta Report which suggests a partial similarity to the Second Vatican Council's references to a "hierarchy of truths."[20]

It is very relevant to our subject then to look at an example from Anglican history of how this principle was evaluated in itself and with respect to dialogue with other Christians. I am thinking here of the ecumenical efforts of William Wake, Archbishop of Canterbury 1716-1737, a man years ahead of his time. In the second lecture we shall take a brief look at Wake's handling of this aspect of our theme of Anglican self-understanding and self-explaining before enquiring whether this raises problems for us today. We can then try to assess such questions as the *via media*, syncretism, the parameters of diversity and the relation to these matters of the established Anglican appeal to Scripture, tradition and reason within a conciliar structure as the means whereby the Spirit maintains the Church in the truth. Accordingly, I leave you with a recent definition of Anglican comprehensiveness by the present Archbishop of Canterbury: "It is the achievement of unity in diversity through the distinction of the essential from the non-essential by means of the Holy Scriptures interpreted by Tradition, in the light of Reason, all expressed in and through the corporate worship of the Church."[21]

2

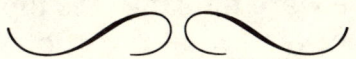

Archbishop Wake and Anglican Self-Understanding in an Ecumenical Context

Our previous concluding thought was of the Anglican understanding and proclamation of the faith and the bearing on this concept of an essential distinction between fundamentals and accessories. What we were thinking of is the demarcation between what is *de fide*, "necessary to salvation," as the sixth of the Thirty-Nine Articles puts it, and what is not an essential element in Christian believing.

Archbishop Wake, who corresponded freely on Christian unity with Reformed theologians such as Jablonski and Turretini as well as with Roman Catholic Gallicans like Du Pin and Girardin, enunciated the same principles to both. The relevant thing for us today is that two centuries ago Anglicanism was explaining itself in an ecumenical context and saying the same thing to the Roman Catholics and to the Reformed.

Proceeding from the basis of the continuity of the Church of England with the Primitive Church in faith[1] and in order,[2] Wake insisted that unity demanded both agreement on fundamentals and acceptance of the distinction between fundamentals and non-essentials as "an indispensable pre-requisite to fruitful discussion of ecclesiastical unity."[3]

In a letter dated 1719 to the Reformed theologian Turretini, the Archbishop set out his philosophy of ecumenism. He had, he said, "come at last to this opinion; that the peace of Christendom can no way be restored but by separating the *fundamental articles* of our religion (in which almost all churches agree) from others, which in their several natures *though not strictly fundamental, may yet be of more, or less, moment to us in the way of our salvation.*" The phrasing here is that of a clearsighted and perceptive theologian, for Wake is not saying that non-essentials could not matter less. On the contrary, it is a question of their nearness to or distance from the fundamentals of Christian faith and this decides their importance. Though by no means an exact parallel it is noteworthy that the Second Vatican Council's decree on ecumenism (11) reads as follows: "When comparing doctrines, they should remember that in Catholic teaching there exists an order or "hierarchy" of truths, since they vary in their relationship to the foundation of the Christian faith." This could yet come to be one of the most creative concepts issuing from that Council. Wake then insisted to his correspondent that "the first being *absolutely* provided for, and *the others which are nearest to them, as much secured as conveniently can be done,* communion should not be broken for the rest, but a prudent liberty be granted to Christians to enjoy their own opinions, without censuring or condemning any that differ from them."[4]

This is an exact and sophisticated setting out of the *rationale* of this distinction and its terms need to be noted with care. It is very far from the casual drawing of a line on one side of which are essentials and on the other side of which are pious opinions which do not greatly matter one way or the other.

Wake made exactly the same points to his Roman Catholic correspondents in France, and always the governing rubric must be, as he wrote to Du Pin, "saving on both sides the faith and verity of the Catholic Church."[5] The theme of Anglican continuity in faith and order with the Primitive Church and that of the distinction between fundamentals and non-essentials keep recurring in the letters to Du Pin and Girardin and are accepted by them.[6] Wake also stresses to Du Pin the position of the three creeds: "These are read in our public services; in these formularies you too along with us profess the Catholic faith; and since in these matters we all agree, in others we ought surely to bear with one another... until such time as God grants that in these matters also we may be of one mind."[7] Writing to Beauvoir, the Anglican Chaplain at Paris who acted as go-between, Wake made the same point: "But then they should in points of doctrine too distinguish fundamentals in which all ought to agree from others of lesser moment, in which error or differences may be tolerated. And I am much mistaken if they must not at last come to the creeds of the four first General Councils, if ever they mean to restore peace to the Church."[8]

This amalgam of stress on the *hapax*, on the fundamentals, on continuity of faith with the Early Church, and on the distinction between fundamentals and non-essentials remains indelibly stamped on Anglican self-understanding and self-explaining. Every aspect of it can be seen, for instance, in the correspondence between Wake's successor in the 1920s, Archbishop Randall Davidson, and Cardinal Mercier. The whole amalgam broke surface throughout the Malines Conversations during that time, and the theme which occasioned the warmest debate at Malines was precisely that of fundamentals and non-fundamentals and the Vincentian Canon. Bishop Charles Gore considered that it was a permanent element in the Anglican position and he insisted to his fellow-conversationalists that "the demand for the distinction... will go on."[9] Not surprisingly, it reappeared in the discussions of the Joint Preparatory Anglican/Roman Catholic Commission in 1968.[10] Before that, the whole position which cements together this cluster of concepts may be clearly discerned in the Bonn Agreement of 1931 between the Church of England and the Old Catholics in whose Declaration of Utrecht (1889) the Vincentian Canon is the ruling idea.

The Bonn Agreement of 1931 had stated: "Intercommunion does not require from either communion the acceptance of all doctrinal opinion, sacramental devotion, or liturgical practice characteristic of the other, but implies that each believes the other to hold all the essentials of the Christian faith." There is incidentally a reflection of this in the *Malta Report* (7).

My last look at Wake brings me firmly into the present and to an examination of how well or how ill this persistent element in Anglicanism has worn. How has it been affected by developments in theology generally and by Biblical criticism? What are the fundamentals and how can you define them today or "Where shall doctrine be found?" as the report just issued of the Doctrinal Commission of the Church of England enquires. Here we are confronting, as Anglican Christians, the many questions about believing in the modern Church and about the corporate nature of faith in our own times.

Wake was anything but naive as a theologian and it comes as no surprise that even in a largely pre-critical period he was totally aware of the difficulty. To Girardin he wrote: "You have remembered rightly and wisely that in treating of articles of evangelical doctrine, fundamentals should be carefully distinguished from non-essentials and matters of greater moment from things of lesser weight.... Neither ought the peace of the Church to be entirely broken for articles of this nature." So far he is reiterating what for him Anglicanism has to say about the unity of the faith to Reformed and Roman Catholic alike. But then he raises the question which theologians and many less specialized believers today are asking when he writes to the French theologian: "It is indeed a work of greater difficulty, not to say danger, to distinguish the essential articles of doctrine from the rest, in such wise that nothing in them is either superfluous or lacking; that nothing essential to salvation is omitted, nor anything non-essential included in the number of essentials."[11] In his letter to Quinot he had gone so far as to say that the fundamentals of faith are "clearly revealed in holy Scripture" and that the three credal summaries "sufficed to define the catholic faith in the first five centuries of the Church."[12] But what he is suggesting to Girardin is that, while this is true, there is more to it in practice in that fundamentals, *still scripturally revealed,* may yet require more amplification than the creeds afford. Otherwise, why is the distinguishing of fundamentals from the rest "a work of greater difficulty"?

The What and the Where of Fundamentals

I have my own view as to a way into this vital area but first let us see how the problem presents itself to others today. Stephen Sykes has an interesting analysis of the Lambeth paragraphs on comprehensiveness and with some of his criticisms I would concur.[13] As he sees it there are three elements in the Conference's statement of 1968: namely, "the affirmation of a comprehensiveness limited and qualified by agreement on fundamentals"; "the assertion that Anglicanism contains within itself both protestant and catholic elements, which will, in the continuing search for the whole truth, one day be completely reconciled" and "the view that there is a development in the apprehension of the truth."[14] With much of Sykes's critique I would find myself in agreement—particularly in his insistence that Anglicanism has "a distinctive standpoint and a distinctive way of communicating that standpoint."[15] This, of course, is very different from saying that Anglicanism has a confessional stance in the sense of the Continental "confessions." This distinction is not made sufficiently clear in his book. As compared with the Thirty-Nine Articles, the latter have a very different context and role, as Thomas Wright has noted, in that they "in some sense are held actually to create and define the Churches which 'confess' them."[16] This is what Archbishop Wake meant by "systems" when he wrote to a correspondent "as to your question about a system of divinity suitable to pupils, I know of none that I could recommend. *Our Church stands upon a different bottom from most of those in which the system-writers have been bred.*"[17] Indeed, during his exchange of letters with reformed theologians concerning the *Forumla Consensus* and the *Confessio Helvetica*, Wake had adhered to the classical Anglican viewpoint and had also written about the distinction between fundamentals and non-essentials in relation to the achieving of unity. His view of the Thirty-Nine Articles was anything but "confessional" though he clearly regarded them as an essential boundary-marker and "as most agreeable to the Holy Scriptures."[18] Stephen Sykes's *The Integrity of Anglicanism* is intended as a contribution to the necessary exercise of Anglican self-criticism. It is not always easy, however, to take hold with fairness of the author's positive position and purpose because of the negative quality of much of what he has written. He himself admits "that it is mainly critical and destructive",[19] reflecting his personal dissatisfaction with current Anglican apologetic, a dissatisfaction which one has little trouble in sharing at any rate in part. Can Sykes's handling of the matter of fundamentals in relation to comprehensiveness help us, in the setting of today's Church? What and where are the fundamentals or where is doctrine to be found? What, in the phrase of the Bonn Agreement, are "all the essentials of the Christian faith?"

Almost that very sentence, as Sykes relates, was used by Hooker in 1594 when he based the unity of the visible Church in the outward profession of "the essence of Christianity."[20] And what did Hooker mean? "He makes explicity clear that by 'the essence of Christianity' he means the articles of Christian belief given as the *regula fidei* in the works of Irenaeus and Tertullian. These fundamentals are, in effect, the propositions which go to make up the Nicene and Apostles' creeds minus some of the late attempts at precision deriving from the circumstances of the Arian controversy. They constitute, Hooker asserts, the faith which Jesus taught and which has characterized the visible Church from that day to this."[21]

A Crisis for Comprehensiveness?

This is where, in Sykes's view, the contemporary crisis of comprehensiveness is at its most acute. If I have grasped his position it may be summarized like this: the use of the distinction between fundamentals and non-fundamentals as a means of establishing comprehensiveness is no longer valid in the form affirmed by Hooker and by Anglicans through the centuries because "modern theologians" question the identification of the faith taught by Christ with that of the *regula fidei* or the fourth-century creeds. He asserts that the validity of the distinction is further impaired because "there would be many who would question whether . . . the faith of those early centuries could be understood and believed by modern man in the precise way in which it was understood and believed by Christians of those times. Even if the identical words were used, it would certainly be the case that their meanings would have changed.... Moreover it is no doubt for this reason, among others, that Root[22] does not identify the fundamentals with certain articles of the creed, but with 'the Nicene faith.' For in this way of expressing the fundamentals there need be no claim that one particular set of statements with fixed and unalterable meanings embodies that faith."[23]

Here we should stand back for a moment and remind ourselves of the objects of the exercise which are to establish where doctrine is to be found and what constitutes the fundamentals which are essential to the Anglican concept of comprehensiveness. Sykes too is deeply concerned about Anglican integrity and seeks answers to the same questions. But does the position of certain "way-out" theologians (one of whom is reported as having, with commendable honesty, resigned his Orders) impair the integrity of the Anglican position? Is not that position clearly set out in our formularies? Does anyone, wishing to establish the doctrinal stance of the Roman Catholic Church on the Incarnation do so by drawing attention to, say, Raymond E. Brown's treatment of the infancy narratives, valuable though this may be in itself?[24]

Sykes believes that Anglican integrity is impaired because, as a result of biblical and historical criticism the Anglican Church "has progressively shed its distinctive confessional commitment."[25] Is this true? If I understand him correctly, he holds that it is so because although the 1975 form of assent "reads as a rather firm profession of faith, it could not be said to exclude a very liberal interpretation. If that is so, then it is vital to add that the same is true of the Church's corporate profession of faith."[26] He appears to have arrived at this conclusion by putting together the 1975 Declaration of Assent and the 1976 *Report on Christian Believing.*

Here, one has to say that this method of putting reports of theological commissions and writings of "radical" theologians alongside the formularies of the Church is not to place like beside like as we seek to answer questions about the corporate nature of the Church's faith. Nobody questions that the function of theology is exploratory and investigative as well as illuminative of the richness of the faith "once for all delivered." *The real question is are certain theologians convinced that this faith has in fact been delivered at all?* If they are not so convinced, do they not place themselves outside the category of those whose function and privilege it is to teach and to build up the *koinonia* of "the household of faith"? This hackle-raising problem is not, as the 1981 Doctrine Commission Report indicates, "merely a question of challenging the right to teaching office of those who cannot, even 'generally', give assent to our formularies. It is equally about the tender consciences of those who believe passionately that truth matters, and that if a Church does not do so in some way or other it is wrong for serious Christians to remain within it." What in fact is at issue is the relation of declared doctrine to ecclesiology: "The underlying issues will not go away, and the problem of the two dogmatisms, the one in favor of declared doctrine, the other opposed to it, may well be our modern version of problems faced by our forefathers ever since the Reformation. At its heart, this is a question about the nature of the Church."[27]

The Preface to the 1975 Declaration of Assent reads as follows: "The Church of England is part of the One, Holy, Catholic and Apostolic Church worshipping the one true God, Father, Son and Holy Spirit. It professes the faith uniquely revealed in the Holy Scriptures and set forth in the catholic creeds, which faith the Church is called upon to proclaim afresh in each generation. Led by the Holy Spirit, it has borne witness to Christian truth in its historic formularies, the Thirty-Nine Articles of Religion, *The Book of Common Prayer* and the Ordering of Bishops, Priests and Deacons. In the declaration you are about to make will you affirm your loyalty to this inheritance of faith as your inspiration and guidance under God, in bringing the grace and truth of Christ to this generation and making Him known to those in your care?"

This preface, deriving no doubt from the Report of the 1968 Lambeth Conference,[28] is in the classical line going back to Jewel and is a clear summary of where, for Anglicans, doctrine is to be found. Sykes, however, finds it necessary to put together this official formulary and the 1976 Report of the Doctrine Commission. Since that particular Report contains some "radical" essays (the term is his own) the implication he finds is that an ordinand identifying with any such views "in such a work" can hardly be said to hold a view not consistent with the Church of England.[29] I am not at all sure of the logic here and there is indeed "a distinction between theology and faith." "Belief" he writes "is not said to be in the theological propositions of the creeds, but in the faith 'revealed in' Holy Scripture and 'set forth in' the catholic creeds. Both Scripture and creeds may be said to be *vehicles* of the faith, a faith which, it may be thought, needs to be reformulated in the present. It seems that the precise wording of the Declaration of Assent, though it reads as a rather firm profession of faith, could not be said to exclude a very liberal interpretation. If that is so, then it is vital to add that the same is true of the Church's *corporate* profession of faith." He then asks "Are there then no boundaries to the degree to which the Church of England is prepared to tolerate diversity of doctrinal conviction?"[30]

I must confess that I find the thread here elusive, though I can see that Sykes is leading up to the statement of his positive conviction that the Church of England "has got definite convictions and insists on a high degree of conformity to them"[31] and "has a substantial and quite vigorously enforced discipline, though not so much in the direct area of Church doctrine as in the indirect area of canon law and liturgical order."[32] It is in canon law and pre-eminently in liturgy that there is found the whole ethos and doctrinal basis of the Church and "the regulated framework for the actual life of the Christian community."[33]

This is certainly true, for Anglicanism, in a phrase from the Doctrine Commission's recent report, "regards declared doctrine not in isolation . . . but rather as a part, an essential part, of a wider whole, namely, the worshipping, teaching and witnessing ('confessing'?) life of the Church." The same report goes on to add "If we ask 'Where, within the Church of England, is doctrine to be found?' the answer is twofold. First, it is found precisely within the Church— not on its own, to be looked up and learnt in a vacuum, but as part of the life of

God's people, to be believed and lived by. Secondly, it is found in a variety of written documents."[34] These latter "form a sort of pyramid, with the Bible at the top, then the creeds, then the Articles, and the rest in a less definite order underneath."[35] Thus, amongst the Church of Ireland's canons concerning worship and liturgy, Canon No. 7 states "The preacher shall endeavour with care and sincerity to minister the word of truth according to holy scripture and agreeable to the Articles of Religion and the Book of Common Prayer, to the glory of God and the edification of the people." Nor is this a new idea. At Birmingham in 1890, E. W. Benson, Archbishop of Canterbury, said "Read your Bible by your Prayer Book" and "We are convinced that our Prayer book is the true interpreter" of the Scriptures.[36] In other words, liturgy with its declared doctrinal content is part of the air breathed by the worshipping and serving community.

Diversity, Freedom and Criteria

As one tries to appreciate the reasons for Sykes's disquiet concerning Anglican doctrinal integrity and his apparent unease as to the content and the application of the criterion of "the faith uniquely revealed in the Holy Scriptures and set forth in the Catholic creeds" and witnessed to in the historic Anglican formularies, one is aware of his candid facing of the position created by the writings of some contemporary Anglican theologians. Yet one has to make two points. The first is the question whether Sykes has partly created his own state of anxiety about Anglican doctrinal integrity by placing side by side declared doctrine and the views of those who modify, question or reject the concept of the *hapax* as enshrined, for instance, in the 1975 Declaration of Assent? This is not, ostrich-like, to pretend that there are not those who do not accept certain declared doctrines, but it *is* to deny that Anglicanism does not declare itself doctrinally in its formularies. The current report of the Doctrine Commission quite bluntly faces what nowadays appears to some to be the ungentlemanly question of exclusion, when one of the essayists suggests that "in the not too distant future" a bishop may have to withdraw his license from someone or, in failing to do so, "unchurch" those members of the household of faith who find disloyalty to the Church's declared faith to be intolerable.[37] In the not too distant past (1947), Archbishop Fisher addressing the Convocation of Canterbury on the subject of Bishop Barnes's *The Rise of Christianity* said that if a bishop whose office was to defend and promote "the general doctrines of the Church and their scriptural basis" wrote a book which does not conform to these requirements he excluded himself.[38] Significantly he added "I trust that what I have said, with the full sense of the responsibility of my office, may serve to minimize the harm and give to members of the Church such reassurance as they may need." Like Fisher, Anglicans would say "I would have no trial in this matter," not just because they have an alleged inherent reaction against doctrinal precision, or a strong resentment of legalism invading the intimate personal area of faith. They also happen to have an inbuilt sensitivity to the tension—some would say the necessary tension—between authority and liberty, between the cohesion in truth of the institutional Church and the freedom of the individual conscience. They tend to hope (sometimes with the laziness of euphoria) that truth will prevail through its own power and, on the whole, they shy away from heresy trials, although the nineteenth century is not without Anglican instances of these.

Are we then saying that it is either a question of the unanimous acceptance of identical statements of faith or of getting out? How fares freedom for the Anglican and what sort of freedom are we visualizing?

At this point it is no digression to remind ourselves of that cluster of concepts attaching to the central Anglican appeal to Scripture and the faith of the Primitive Church. These include as well as the stress on continuity in faith and order, a concept of diffused authority in which the appeal to Scripture, tradition and reason plays a part. There is not only the relationship of fundamentals to comprehensiveness but to the legitimate limits of diversity within the unity of faith which raises at once the question of freedom.

Emmanuel Amand de Mendieta, formerly a Benedictine monk, saw this freedom as something which has colored the whole ethos of Anglicanism. He writes movingly of "the spiritual freedom of the individual believer" and claims that "there is no other Church in the Catholic tradition . . . which so passionately believes in spiritual freedom, and which so positively demands it from clergy and laity alike."[39] This was something he discovered from his own experience as an Anglican and it only becomes an idealized mythology if one misinterprets this freedom as a freedom to believe or disbelieve anything one likes and still to call one's self an Anglican. There is this freedom, with all the dangers and loss involved in it, as William Temple pointed out,[40] but which we value as a real part of our Anglican heritage. Yet we know that it has parameters beyond which you cease to be an Anglican. Laud saw this clearly, this human tension between the freedom of the individual believer and the question of his identity as a member of the household of faith. He has no wish to confine Catholicity to what he calls "a narrow conclave." Rather does he seek "to lay open those wider gates of the Catholic Church, confined to no age time or place." But there are parameters—"nor knowing any bounds but that faith which was once, (and but once for all) delivered to the saints."[41]

It is only by recognizing the Scriptures "as its ultimate point of reference (that is, as 'authoritative') which enables the Church to continue as an identifiable society." So goes an essay by Anthony Harvey in the Doctrine Commission's current report, and it touches on the very point which we have been considering: "As an individual I am of course free to believe what I like. . . . But in so far as I am a member of the Church, I associate myself with a 'corporate believing' which consists in a recognition of, and a constantly changing response to, 'the authority of Scripture.' There may be no point at which this ever-moving response to the historic given-ness of Christianity can be caught, immobilized and presented as a still shot, a systematic statement of belief (though an important part of the response itself will consist of personal attempts by theologians to do precisely this.) But this does not prevent any individual who consciously associates himself with the Church from recognising that, by so doing, he is making his own personal understanding of the faith to a certain extent subservient to that collective activity of attention to, and interpretation of, Scripture which is an essential part of corporate believing."[42]

This looks like an honestly dynamic rather than a static approach to the position set out for example in the Declaration of Assent, and to the relationship between the individual's spiritual freedom and the corporate believing of the Family—in other words, to the implications of membership. Does this create a crisis of comprehensiveness *only* if we try to comprehend within the Family those who question that which alone establishes the identity of the Family?[43] Do we then detect, as we reach this point in our reflections, that Anglicanism, officially and actually, permits such "a breadth of doctrinal tolerance of doubt and internal contradiction" as impairs its integrity?[44] Not the least useful aspect of criticisms from within the Family, such as those of Sykes is that one is obliged to look hard at Anglicanism's self-portrayal.

The second point which one would wish to make is accordingly to consider Sykes's treatment of the interpretation of faith which, he fears, permits doubts and contradictions to shelter under the umbrella of a seemingly orthodox declaration of faith, thus calling in question the coherence and integrity of the Anglican Communion.[45]

His point is that in much current orthodox Anglican apologetic "the fundamentals are not said to be the articles of the Nicene or Apostles' creeds; nor even to consist in any particular set of propositions. The fundamental rock of agreement is, nonetheless . . . 'the Nicene faith', that Christ was the incarnate Word of God." This means, Sykes says, that "in this way of expressing the fundamentals there need be no claim that one particular set of statements with fixed and unalterable meanings embodies that faith ."[46] One is tempted to ask whoever said that it did or could? The gravamen here is "if it is not the case that the propositions of the creed of the Council of Nicaea are the fixed and unalterable truths of Christianity nonetheless it is the case, according to this way of thinking, that the faith which came to expression in what was said by the orthodox fathers at Nicaea constitutes the fundamentals of any form of Christianity with a claim to be Christian. Thus it follows that the propositional form of the 'Nicene faith' is, in this more indirect sense, paradigmatic; and this too is a position which at least some Anglican theologians could feel constrained to deny, and for the same reasons as were brought against the earlier, less sophisticated version of the theory."[47]

Now I certainly do not for a moment suggest that Sykes is a prisoner, or wants anyone else to be a prisoner, of some form of a propositional concept of revelation. Nor would I wish to go to the other extreme which suggests that in this area propositions are valueless and event is all. Events have to be communicated and communication is through words which are always an approximation and never totally complete. It does seem to me that any overstressing of the propositional aspect (indicating how this excludes "at least some Anglican theologians") results in overweighting and upsetting the delicate balance of formulation and meaning. For it is basically a question of meanings and the forms for expressing meanings which is at the heart of the dogmatic exercise. All the time it is a question of the inherent limitations of language to express, let alone to encapsulate, the richness of the given faith in its totality. All the time it is a question of the living interaction of that *hapax* on the interpretations which it requires and which at the same time it delimits. The phrase of Pope John XXIII at the opening of the Second Vatican Council is not without relevance here: "The substance of the ancient doctrine of the deposit of faith is one thing, and the way in which it is presented is another."

As we look at the questions, What are the fundamentals of the faith?, and, Where is doctrine to be found?, it would appear to many of us that the interpretation and restatement of "the Nicene faith" is a part of that ever-moving response to the historical given-ness of Christianity which is the living tradition of the living Church in action. The governing rubric here for Anglicans has always been that of the consonance of this ongoing exercise of interpretation with Scripture. Several New Testament Christologies and the several interpretations of them in the Primitive Church lie behind the Nicene statement of the mystery of Christ which has to be proclaimed to each age in its own idiom. This position has, incidentally, been firmly and sensitively set out in *Believing in the Church:* "The essential thing is rather that the Church should be seen to be remaining faithful to the authenticity of Scripture, as mediated by its historic tradition, and to express this faithfulness by a constant wrestling with the problems involved in discovering the force and relevance of the biblical story to the circumstances of Christianity to-day."[48]

A contemporary exposition of this approach to declared doctrine and its interpretation is to be found in the Venice Statement on Authority in the Church: "All generations and cultures must be helped to understand that the good news of salvation is also for them. *It is not enough for the Church simply to repeat the original apostolic words. It has also prophetically to translate them in order that the hearers in their situation may understand and respond to them. All such restatement must be consonant with the apostolic witness recorded in the Scriptures; for in this witness the preaching and teaching of ministers, and statements of local and universal councils, have to find their ground and consistency.* Although these clarifications are conditioned by the circumstances which prompted them, some of their perceptions may be of lasting value. In this process the Church itself may come to see more clearly the implications of the gospel. This is why the Church has endorsed certain formulas as authentic expressions of its witness, whose significance transcends the setting in which they were first formulated. *This is not to claim that these formulas are the only possible, or even the most exact, way of expressing the faith, or that they can never be improved.* Even when a doctrinal definition is regarded by the Christian community as part of its permanent teaching, this does not exclude subsequent restatement. Although the categories of thought and the mode of expression may be superseded, *restatement always builds upon, and does not contradict, the truth intended by the original definition.*"[49]

That would certainly represent my faith as an Anglican and I suspect it would satisfy most members of the Church. If it excludes "certain modern theologians" then so be it, or, as the Doctrine Report observes in a similar context "If this causes problems, they are problems that the Church has declared that she intends to live with."[50] While obviously I do not attach the same weight to many of his points that he does, I have stayed with Stephen Sykes's criticisms from within the Anglican household because, like medicinal astringents, they can produce a healing smart and sting. Our self-portrait ought not to ignore the existence of a certain tendency to theological complacency which can become quite Panglossian, tacitly assuming that all is for the best in the best of all possible Churches. Nevertheless, I do not see the Anglican doctrinal stance as impaired in its integrity for the reasons adduced in these lectures. Freed from the burden of theological ideologies[51] (we have never been Hookerians or Cranmerians) Anglicanism has continued to proclaim "the faith uniquely revealed in the Holy Scriptures and set forth in the catholic creeds, *which faith the Church is called upon to proclaim afresh in each generation.*"

What this is saying is, as the Doctrine Commission's report indicated,[52] that

Scripture, tradition and the *lex orandi* provide a criterion for membership without which what we have is not the household of faith but a theological debating society. But within that living circle of declaration and faith-response there is a liberty of which Anglicans have no need to be ashamed as they wrestle with the tensions created by biblical and credal criticism. As the passage from the Lambeth Conference definition of 1968 which constituted our starting point notes: "Comprehensiveness implies a willingness to allow liberty of interpretation, with a certain slowness in arresting or restraining exploratory thinking."

Epilogue

What then was Archbishop Wake getting at when he asserted that the fundamentals were "clearly revealed in holy Scripture" and that the creeds "sufficed to define the catholic faith," but that it was still difficult to distinguish the essentials from the non-essentials so that "nothing essential to salvation is omitted"? In effect, as I think can be seen from his correspondence with Du Pin especially in connection with the latter's *Commonitorium*, I hold that he was saying that other things beside apostolic faith were essential to the true being of the Church and that these were Scripturally warranted as essentials in the life of Christianity. These were the sacraments and a ministry to administer them (which he saw as a threefold ministry) and the continued offering of life-creative worship within the household of faith. He was simply stating what Anglicanism had maintained before him in its formularies and liturgy and in the writings of its theologians, namely, that without Baptism, without the Book and the Bread, without a Ministry, there could be no Church. It seems, therefore, that fundamentals include that without which the household of faith could have no existence. In other words, can one see an Anglican (or most other Christians) saying that the Church can exist without apostolic faith and order, the dominical sacraments and the worship which builds up the individual within the common life of the Body of Christ? Is this then the area in which Wake saw difficulty in distinguishing "the essential articles of doctrine from the rest, in such wise that nothing in them is either superfluous or lacking; that nothing essential to salvation is omitted, nor anything non-essential included in the number of essentials"? Are baptism and the eucharist not fundamentals?

Whether I am correct in believing that this is what Wake had in mind at this point or not, the suggestion is certainly in tune with the ecclesiology and the view of Christianity which his letters developed so fully. It is then very relevant as we enquire about fundamentals to see how the New Testament bears on this approach. The elements constitutive of the Church are seen in Acts 2:41-2[53] as baptism, the apostolic faith, the breaking of bread, the *koinonia* and worship. The witness of the epistles in general shows baptism through the one Spirit as the one entrance to the one Body, the fellowship of one Lord, one faith, one baptism. The eucharist is the very form of the unity of that fellowship —"we are one bread, one body." The Church is "the household of faith" within which there is an ordained ministry to serve the priesthood of all the faithful. This ministry equips God's people for service and builds up the body of Christ so that the members may attain a personal maturity of which Christ is the measure, and this is a chief goal of belonging to the *koinonia*. To this is related as a means to an end the specific worship of the fellowship, a ministry of the Word and Sacrament, as the first description of a Christian Sunday morning testifies.[54] No matter how we dissect all this in terms of authorship, dating, sources and destinations, it can hardly be disputed that the identity of the Church from those earliest times was seen as inextricably and essentially bound up with apostolic faith, the sacraments, ministry and worship focussing on building up a common life in and through the risen Lord so that the members live through his life transmitted to them as they receive and respond in faith to the Gospel of God. One recalls also the ecclesial reality emerging from the letters of Ignatius where, as well as the one saving faith in the Word made flesh, the one eucharist and the one ministry are clearly regarded as fundamental to the being of the Church ("Without these there is no Church deserving of the name," Trallians, III). Written under the near shadow of martyrdom (between A.D. 110-117), the Ignatian letters tell us much about the household of faith and its beliefs in the Roman province of Asia at a time when some men were alive who could have remembered the apostles. It helps the perspective if one remembers that these letters are roughly contemporary with the Pastoral Epistles, and a couple of decades later than Acts, unless one accepts John Robinson's earlier dating of some of the New Testament books.[55]

After this lecture was written, there came to hand an interesting instance of the spontaneous combustion of similar ideas in a different context on the other side of the Atlantic.

The report of the current Lutheran-Episcopal dialogue in the United States lays stress on apostolicity as the Church's continuity with Christ and the apostles in its movement through history. It takes its description of "the dynamic, diverse reality of apostolicity or apostolic succession" from the elements included in the same text, Acts 2:42, to which I have made reference. It further comments on developments of this apostolicity which "continue to shape the Church's faith, life and mission today." The relevance of the forms of apostolicity noted in the following extract from the report to what we have been saying with regard to what Wake called "the number of the essentials" is clear. It derives added force as comment surfacing from an actual contemporary dialogue between Anglicans and Lutherans.

"Three forms of apostolicity emerge in the early Church especially directed towards the threat of the Gnostics in the areas of (1) doctrine, (2) worship and (3) order.

(1) The canon of prophetic and apostolic Scripture is set as the recognized authoritative norm or rule of doctrine. Apostolic 'rules of faith' in credal form develop, not only to guard against heresy and to instruct catechumens but also (2) for use in baptismal liturgies as interrogatory creeds or as summaries of the faith for the newly baptized. Concomitant with this was the development of influential liturgies which helped protect apostolic authenticity in the celebration of Word and Sacrament. (3) Apostolic succession was wedded to succession of bishops in sees so that bishops were looked to as guardians of apostolic faith and practice, representing the teaching authority of the apostles" (*Lutheran-*

Episcopal Dialogue: Reports and Recommendations, Second Series, Cincinnati, 1981, pp. 32-33).

In other words, for the Church to be recognizably the Church its apostolicity must be clearly evident and the elements which constitute apostolicity are therefore essential to its being and to its proclamation of the Gospel. It seems therefore that these Scripturally warranted elements must be included in the fundamentals.

A fundamental is, by definition, a principle which serves as groundwork for a system, or as the base from which other aspects derive. If we take Scripture as "a normative record of the authentic foundation of the faith" and as the reference point for the Church's faith and practice, to say nothing of being the vehicle by which "the authority of the Word of God is conveyed,"[56] it seems unavoidable that we look again at the content we give to the concept of fundamentals. Is belief in the Church not part of the Gospel and hence of the creeds? Have we forgotten that the Church is very much part of what is "revealed in the Scriptures and set forth in the catholic creeds," although the preface to the Declaration of Assent has not forgotten: "The Church of England is part of the One, Holy, Catholic and Apostolic Church worshipping the one true God, Father, Son and Holy Spirit." If the Church is then the eucharistic fellowship of those who are baptized and profess the apostolic faith by which through grace they strive to live out their discipleship as followers of Jesus, the Lord, what does this tell us about fundamentals?

Can we doubt, knowing his letters, that for Wake, baptism, eucharist, ministry and worship as well as apostolic faith, would be classified as what he called "essentials"? At any rate, this would seem to be the thinking of the Chicago-Lambeth Quadrilateral which has passed through a variety of formulations between 1888 and 1968. Its four essentials for unity—the Scriptures, the Creeds, the dominical sacraments, and a commonly acknowledged ministry, largely match the elements constitutive of the Church in Acts and the Epistles. Do these comprise, or do they not, the base which constitutes the household of faith as an identifiable society? Without them would the Church be recognizable as "Church"?[57] Anglican formularies from the Thirty-Nine Articles of 1571 to the Preamble to the 1870 Constitution of the Church of Ireland and to the Church of Englands' 1975 Declaration of Assent do not think so, and therefore, I submit, we are mistaken if we limit the concept of fundamentals so as to exclude what the credal summaries include by clear implication when immediately after the Trinitarian affirmations it lists belief in the One, Holy Catholic and Apostolic Church.

Let me close this overly lengthy lecture by asserting by way of postscript that I do not believe in the Anglican synthesis. I do believe in the Anglican symbiosis. To synthesize means to build up separate positions into a connected whole. This is what the Lambeth Conference Report of 1968, already quoted on comprehensiveness, was implying: "It has been the tradition of Anglicanism to contain within one body both Protestant and Catholic elements. But there is a continuing search for the whole truth in which these elements will find complete reconciliation." This piece of wishful thinking about a happy future synthesis typifies a certain kind of careless Anglican theological euphoria at its worst. It is completely shallow, and what is more, untrue.

Symbiosis, on the other hand, means the permanent union between organisms each of which depends for its existence on the other. I believe in the Anglican symbiosis, the unity of faith in which the Catholic and Reformed elements are necessary to one another because both are essential and integral elements in the one Gospel of God. Let Michael Ramsey have the last word: "The Anglican Church is committed not to a vague position wherein the Evangelical and the Catholic views are alternatives, but to the Scriptural faith wherein both elements are of one. . . . If the meaning of the Anglican Church is thus sought in terms of the Church of the New Testament, then none of the cries of partisans can ever interpret it aright."[58]

Or perhaps one ought to say "the second last word." In a recent book, two well-known Anglican theologians, the Hanson brothers, commented at the close of their survey of the Christian faith on the task and methodology of the Anglican theologian and on the nature of Anglicanism. The first comment is confirmatory of our approach in these lectures to the way in which their "inheritance of faith" (to use the phrase from the Declaration of Assent) impels and requires Anglicans to do theology: "We hope that the book itself adequately illustrates what we conceive to be the task of an Anglican theologian: Christian belief must be justified in terms of the witness of the Bible, of the history of Christian tradition (i.e., the theology which Christians have written since New Testament times up till the present day), and of what our own reason can tell us. None of these three elements must be regarded as infallible or in itself decisive, but none can safely be ignored.

We have, perhaps arrogantly, claimed that this is a characteristically Anglican approach. But if it is regarded as an *exclusively* Anglican approach it will have failed in its objective. Our hope is that this will become increasingly the ecumenical way of writing theology."

The second comment expresses a hope and a conviction in line with the main theme which these lectures have endeavored to set out. It may suitably serve as *envoi* to the subject of "The Unity of Anglicanism: Catholic and Reformed" since it looks not only inward on Anglican self-understanding but outward on the ecumenical vocation of all Christians: "We only wish to continue calling ourselves Anglicans (itself a restrictive name—the whole Church can never be Anglican any more than it can be Roman) until the time comes when all Christian theologians can unite as Catholic Christians, not Roman Catholic or Anglo-Catholic, not even as Protestant or Evangelical, but merely as Catholics who, just because they are Catholic, are also evangelical."[59]

NOTES

-1-

1 *The Nature of the Lion* (London 1962) by J. P. Hodges.

2 See the *Preamble and Declaration* prefixed to the Constitution of the Church of Ireland, the Introduction and I (1)-(3.)

3 J. P. Hodges, loc. cit., pp. 85-6.

4 Ibid. and cp. *An Apology of the Church of England*, Part VI, C. XVI, "We are come, as near as we possibly could, to the church of the apostles and of the old catholic bishops and fathers." For a discussion of the probability of Jewel having had the assistance of others in producing the *Apology*, which certainly had an "official" aura for contemporaries, see John E. Booty, *John Jewel as an Apologist for the Church of England*, (London: SPCK, 1963), pp. 45-55.

5 J. P. Hodges, loc. cit., p. 86, and cp. Strype, *Annals*, II, 148.

6 *The One Way of Composing the Differences on Foot*, Works, (1854 ed.) V, 29.

7 Loc. cit., especially C. XIII, "Ecclesia Anglicana."

8 *A Relation of the Conference* (3rd ed.), Preface

9 Loc. cit., pp. 28, 32, 34.

10 *The Gospel and the Catholic Church* (London: Longman, Green and Co. Ltd., 1936,) p. 209.

11 Loc. cit., p. 208.

12 Loc. cit., p. 209.

13 See *"The Spirit of Anglicanism"* (New York: Charles Scribners Sons 1965,) by H. R. McAdoo, passim, for an analysis of this theological method and its place in Anglicanism.

14 *Renewal in Worship,* by M. E. Marshall in *SEARCH: A Church of Ireland Journal,* Vol 4, Number one, Spring 1981, p. 9.

15 *The Anglican Synthesis,* (Derby: Peter Smith, 1964,) ed. W. R. F. Browning, p. 139.

16 "Rome and Canterbury—Unity, Diversity and Comprehensiveness," given at Westminster Abbey, March 11, 1981 and circulated through the Church Information Office.

17 *The Lambeth Conference 1968: Resolutions and Reports,* pp. 140-141.

18 (London: SPCK, 1978) Chapter I, "The Crisis of Anglican Comprehensiveness."

19 *The Malta Report,* being the report of the Anglican/Roman Catholic Joint Preparatory Commission. (London: SPCK, 1974).

20 *The Malta Report,* (6.)

21 The Archbishop of Canterbury's Lenten Address at Westminster Abbey on Wednesday, March 11, 1981 (C.I.O.)

-2-

1 The comparison of the Church of England with the Primitive Church should be "cum constitutione, fide, regimine ecclesiae catholicae secundi, tertii aut etiam quarti saeculi." So wrote Wake to Du Pin. *(William Wake,* Cambridge: Cambridge University Press, 1957, by Norman Sykes, Vol. I p. 259).

2 "We rightly claim for ourselves an uninterrupted succession of these; and we are prepared to prove this clearly": Wake to Du Pin (loc. cit. ib.).

3 *William Wake*, I, p. 254.

4 *William Wake*, I, p. 253.

5 *William Wake*, I, p. 272.

6 *William Wake*, I, pp. 264-5.

7 *William Wake*, I, p. 259.

8 *William Wake*, I, p. 264 and similarly, two years later, in a letter to Quinot, ib., p. 297.

9 See, *The Conversations at Malines* (1927) pp. 38, 40.

10 See, *The Malta Report*, 6 (1968).

11 *William Wake*, I, pp. 262-3.

12 *William Wake*, I, p. 297.

13 Stephen W. Sykes, *The Integrity of Anglicanism* (Oxford: A. R. Mowbray and Co. Ltd., 1978) pp. 10-24.

14 Loc. cit., p. 10.

15 Loc. cit., p. 73 and cp. my *"The Spirit of Anglicanism"* (New York: Charles Scribners Sons, 1965).

16 *Believing in the Church* (Wilton, CT: Morehouse-Barlow Co., 1982) p. 123.

17 *William Wake*, I, p. 163.

18 *William Wake*, II, pp. 32-3: "We have left everyone to interpret them in his own sense; and they are indeed so generally framed, that they may, without an equivocation, have more senses than one fairly put upon them" and "It was for the same reason that King Charles I caused the 39 Articles to be republished by his authority, with the famous declaration before them, forbidding private persons to interpret

them in any one determinate sense of their own imposing; and requiring all subscribers to do it in the general words of the Articles. . . . And our most eminent divines have many of them thought, and even declared it in writing, that these Articles were designed by the Church rather as articles of public peace, and to *set bounds* to men's preaching or writing or instructing the people, than as doctrinal points to be professedly believed by every minister of our Church . . ." (Letter of 24 February 1718 to Turrettini).

[19] *The Integrity of Anglicanism* (Oxford: A. R. Mowbray and Co. Ltd., 1978) p. 87.

[20] Loc. cit., p. 11.

[21] Ibid.

[22] He has been discussing a letter of Professor H. E. Root in which the latter maintains that "the Nicene faith" constitutes the fundamentals, ibid. p. 12.

[23] Ibid. p. 13.

[24] *The Birth of the Messiah* (Garden City, NY: Doubleday and Co., 1977,) by Raymond E. Brown, S. S.

[25] Ibid. pp. 42-3.

[26] Ibid. p. 38.

[27] *Believing in the Church* (Wilton, CT.: Morehouse-Barlow Co., 1981) pp. 139-140.

[28] *The Lambeth Conference 1968: Resolutions and Reports*, p. 82.

[29] Loc. cit., p. 37.

[30] Ibid. p. 38.

[31] Ibid. p. 43.

[32] Ibid. p. 44.

[33] Ibid. pp. 45-8.

[34] *Believing in the Church* (Wilton, CT.: More-

house-Barlow Co., 1981), pp. 110-115.

35 Loc. cit. p. 112.

36 *Edward White Benson* (1899) by A. C. Benson, Vol. II, p. 683.

37 *Believing in the Church* (Wilton, CT.: Morehouse-Barlow Co., 1981), p. 140 and cp. the Dean of Norwich's comments in *The Church Times*, p. 11 (6-11-81).

38 "The Bishop of Birmingham may be satisfied that his teaching in this book conforms to these requirements. I would have no trial in this matter: but I must say, for my part, that I am not so satisfied. If his views were mine, I should not feel that I could still hold episcopal office in the Church." *Fisher of Lambeth* (1969), by William Purcell, p. 167.

39 *Anglican Vision* (London: SPCK, 1971), by Emmanuel Amand de Mendieta, p. 63.

40 W. Temple, *Essays in Christian Politics* (London: Longmans, Green & Co., Ltd., 1927), pp. 201-2.

41 *A Relation of the Conference*, Preface.

42 *Believing in the Church* (Wilton, CT.: Morehouse-Barlow, Co., 1981), pp. 43-44. Sykes does point out that "a lot of liberal thinking . . . is parasitic on the positive convictions of those who are clearer and more definite about what they believe" (loc. cit., p. 43).

43 "The relationship of the believer and his Church to Scripture, and the authority ascribed to it and to tradition, appear to offer a criterion by which we may pronounce whether he and his denomination are members of the Church," *Believing in the Church*, p. 43.

44 *The Integrity of Anglicanism*, (Oxford: A. R.

Mowbray, 1978) p. 51.

45 Ibid., pp. 37, 44.

46 Ibid., pp. 12-13.

47 Ibid., and cp. pp. 37-8, 42-3.

48 *Believing in the Church,* p. 39, and cp. the following: "In all the historic churches a Christain is never bound only to the original history-with-interpretation offered by Scripture; he has also to acknowledge his debt to the subsequent tradition of interpretation inherited by the denomination in which he finds himself. In this sense he recognizes the 'authority' of tradition" (Ibid. p. 42) and "In all these cases the relationship of the believer and his church to Scripture, and the authority ascribed to it and to tradition, appear to offer a criterion by which we may pronounce whether he or his denomination are members of the Church." (Ibid. p. 43).

49 *Authority in the Church (1976),* 15. Statement of the Anglican/Roman Catholic International Commission.

50 Loc. cit., p. 134.

51 The phrase is Emmanuel Amand de Mendieta's in an essay contributed to *The Anglican Synthesis* (Derby: Peter Smith, 1964), p. 137.

52 Loc. cit., p. 43, pp. 141-143.

53 "Then they that gladly received his word were baptized . . . and they continued stedfastly in the apostles' doctrine and fellowship, and in the breaking of bread, and in prayers," Acts 2: 41-42.

54 "And upon the first day of the week, when the disciples came together to break bread, Paul preached unto them", Acts 20:7.

55 *Redating the New Testament* (1976), John A. T. Robinson.

56 cp. *Authority in the Church, 2* (ARCIC, 1976).

57 cp. *Believing the Church*, p. 140.

58 *The Gospel and the Catholic Church* (London: Longman, Green and Co. Ltd., 1936), p. 209.

59 *Reasonable Belief: A Survey of the Christain Faith* (Oxford, 1980) by A. T. Hanson and R. P. C. Hanson, p. 265.

BIBLIOGRAPHY

Booty, John E., *John Jewel as an Apologist for the Church of England*, London: SPCK, 1963.

Brown, Raymond E., *The Birth of the Messiah*, Garden City, N.Y.: Doubleday and Co., 1977.

Browning, W. R. F., ed., *The Anglican Synthesis*, Derby: Peter Smith, 1964.

de Mendieta, Emmanuel Amand, *Anglican Vision*, London: SPCK, 1971.

Hanson, A. T. and R. P. C. Hanson, *Reasonable Belief: A Survey of the Christian Faith*, Oxford: 1980.

The Lambeth Conference 1968: Resolutions and Reports, London: SPCK, 1978.

The Malta Report published in: Alan C. Clark Colin Davey, ed., *Anglican/Roman Catholic Dialogue: The Work of the Preparatory Commission*, London: SPCK, 1974.

McAdoo, Henry R. and Alan Clark, ed., *The Final Report*, Anglican-Roman Catholic International Commission, London: SPCK and Cincinnati: Forward Movement Publications, 1982.

McAdoo, Henry R., *The Spirit of Anglicanism*, New York City: Charles Scribners Sons, 1965.

Ramsey, Arthur Michael, *The Gospel and the Catholic Church*, London: Longmans, Green & Co., Ltd., 1936.

Robinson, John A. T., *Redating the New Testament*, Philadelphia: The Westminster Press, 1976.

Sykes, Norman, *William Wake, Archbishop of Canterbury*, Cambridge: Cambridge University Press, 1957.

Sykes, Stephen, *The Integrity of Anglicanism*, Oxford: A. R. Mowbray and Co., Ltd., 1978.

Taylor, John V., ed., *Believing in the Church*, Wilton, CT: Morehouse Barlow Co., Inc., 1982.

Temple, William, *Essays in Christian Politics and Kindred Subjects*, London: Longmans, Green & Co., Ltd., 1927.